Noche de Colibríes: Ekphrastic Poems

Xánath Caraza

Translated by Stephen Holland-Wempe

ISBN-10: 1940856027
ISBN-13: 978-1-940856-02-5

Library of Congress Control Number: 2013923268

DEDICATION

Para

Rafaela   Mariana

Emilio   Xiuh

Ollin.

… La canción del sol
está hecha de luz
luz
    luz
        luz…
…Sol,
oh, sílaba amarilla.

Homero Aridjis

Contents

ACKNOWLEDGMENTS

Thank you to the editors of literary journals, anthologies, websites, in which some of the poems of this volume have appeared.

"Miel" in *Círculo de Poesía*
"Árbol de poesía" in *Revista Zona de Ocio*
"Sombras" in *Círculo de Poesía, Luces y Sombras V. 28* and *Runaway Pony an Anthology of Verse After Paintings by Thomas Pecore Weso*
"Shadows" in *Runaway Pony an Anthology of Verse After Paintings by Thomas Pecore Weso*
"Last Blue Moon" in *To the Stars through Difficulties*
"Nocturno" *in Runaway Pony an Anthology of Verse After Paintings by Thomas Pecore Weso*
"Nocturne" *in Runaway Pony an Anthology of Verse After Paintings by Thomas Pecore Weso*
"Yanga" in *Corazón Pintado: Ekphrastic Poems, Conjuro, Revista Zona de Ocio, SonSomos.com, Ensemble*
"Sonido" in *Círculo de poesía.*

NOCHE DE COLIBRÍES

Para The Galactic Tree of Life, the Story of Everything de Heriberto Luna

Vuelan los colibríes sobre
Las ensortijadas ramas
Filigrana de ámbares como frutos nacen

Navegan los árboles a la deriva
Uno a uno, gotas de poesía,
Ópalos en la oscuridad

Pequeñas lunas vibran
Con el viento de altamar
Su sonido inhalan las mariposas

Titilantes estrellas rodean
Al flameante árbol de lunas
Que se mece, se mece, se mece en el mar

Noche de colibríes
Espíritus de los ancestros
Se alimentan de la bermeja savia

Entre las ramas fluye
La poesía de Mesoamérica
De la boca de la luna emerge

Con el vaivén del mar y
Las constelaciones de diamantes
Viperinas lenguas sisean pasión

NIGHT OF HUMINGBIRDS

After The Galactic Tree of Life, the Story of Everything by
Heriberto Luna

Hummingbirds take flight to
Curled branches
Filigree in amber as fruit is born

Trees navigate drifting
One by one, droplets of poetry,
Opals in darkness

Slight moons quiver
Due to wind from open sea,
Butterflies inhale the wind's wailing

Glimmering stars surround
Blazing tree of moons
Rocking back and forth at sea, back and forth, back and forth

Night of hummingbirds
Spirits of the ancestors
Are nourished on vermillion sap

Through the branches,
Mesoamerican poetry flows
From the moon's mouth, it emerges

By virtue of swaying on the sea and
Diamond constellations,
Snake-like tongues hiss passion

Xánath Caraza

MIEL

Para La flor de guayaba de Israel Nazario

En la brisa del jardín
agita sus alas el lapislázuli.
Diminuto sonsonete esparce
la nacarada luz del amanecer.

Blanca flor seductora,
invita a probar su miel, se dilata
con el rocío de la mañana.
Perfume entretejido con la humedad.

Densa atmósfera azul
custodia al guayabo de malaquita.
Destellos de luz emanan
de las alas del colibrí.

Música suave se impregna
en el pistilo de la flor
con el primer contacto, entonces
chupa delicadamente la miel.

HONEY

After La flor de guayaba by Israel Nazario

In the garden's mist
lapis lazuli beats it wings.
Pint-size fluttering spans out
Pearly, dawn light

White, seductive flower
beckons for a taste of her honey, offering herself
with morning dew
Perfume entwined with moisture

Thick, blue atmosphere
Guardian guava tree of malachite
Shimmer of light smolders
from the hummingbird's wings

Soft music drenches
the flower's pistil
with first contact, then
delicately draws up the honey

DEL TRONCO HERIDO

Para Madre de Juan Chawuk

De entre las hojas emerges
Canción de árboles
Aroma sensual que vuela hasta
Los poros de mi piel
Susurro verde de la noche
Y llanto carmín de la aurora
Llamado a vivir
De la piel brota la vida
Del cuerpo nace la esperanza
Con la llama de jade en flor
Se protegen los árboles
Con la púrpura humedad
Se resguarda la raíz
Del tronco herido
Brota la esperanza

FROM THE WOUNDED TREE TRUNK

After Mother by Juan Chawuk

Jutting out from budding leaflets,
Song of trees
Sensual fragrance which stretches to
The pores of my skin
Green nighttime murmuring
And crimson wailing from the glowing light
Called to live
Out of my skin, life blazes forward
Out of my body, hope is brought about
By a jade-torched flower,
The trees are shielded
By purple moisture,
The roots are sheltered
From the wounded tree trunk,
Hope sprouts

Xánath Caraza

LOS NADADORES

Para Amanecer andalusí de Adriana Manuela

Los nadadores se entierran
después de perder sus sueños
en sus pequeños espacios.
Para unos, cambia la esencia,
otros, renacen como árboles
en la dureza de la soledad.
Algunos, sin pensarlo,
sólo buscan la luz y la esperanza.
En el policromado cielo del atardecer
confunden el sol con sus deseos.
Proyectan en la bóveda celeste
la intensidad de sus miradas,
el secreto de su existencia.
Los nadadores vuelan hasta
las profundidades de sus sueños.
No se intimidan frente al aroma
del último atardecer.

SWIMMERS

After Amanecer andalusí by Adriana Manuela

Swimmers interred
after their dreams slip through their fingers
in their undersized plots.
For several, their lifeblood adjusts.
For others, they are reborn as trees
as they endure loneliness.
A good few, without question,
only seek light and hope.
Up in the multicolored sky at dusk,
they muddle the sun with longing.
They forcefully cast their staring
onto the otherworldly vaulted crypt,
riddle of their existence.
Swimmers take flight to
the depths of their dreams.
They are not daunted by facing the whiff
of their only remaining dusk.

Xánath Caraza

ÁRBOL DE POESÍA

Para La integración de la vida de Juan Chawuk

Si los árboles azules diesen poesía
Este árbol sería uno de ellos

Si las hojas del otoño fuesen versos
Cuántas cubrirían mis pasos

Si los troncos milenarios fuesen lingüística
Este sería el más elaborado

Si las semillas del desierto fuesen rimas
Cuántas estuviesen germinando

Si el polen amarillo fuese ritmo
La atmósfera vibraría con el viento

TREE OF POEMS

After La integración de la vida by Juan Chawuk

Were blue trees to recite poetry,
This tree would be one

Were autumn leaves to be verses,
An abundance would cover my path

Were millennium tree trunks to be linguistics,
This tree would be richly ornate

Were desert seeds to be rhymes,
Multitudes would be sprouting

Were yellow pollen to be rhythm,
The atmosphere would pulsate with wind

SOMBRAS

Para Red Fence de Tom Weso Pecore

Pasión es sombra en el desierto
Que llega esporádicamente
Calmando la sed

Desierto rojo
Desde el balcón de madera
Rocas escarpadas en la piel

Calor que golpea el cuerpo
Tornado de fuego que envuelve
Aspiro el atardecer

Aire rojo
Cascada de fuego
Paisaje que quema

Pasión es desierto rojo
Que se desliza desde mis pies
Que dé tregua

SHADOWS

After Red Fence by Tom Pecore Weso

Passion is a shadow in the desert
Which sporadically turns up
Quenching my thirst

Scarlet desert
From a timber gallery
Sheer hoodoos next to my skin

Warmth that strikes my body
Blazing tornado which shrouds
Gasping for the twilight

Crimson air
Firestorm cascade
Landscape on fire

Passion is a red desert
Which slips away from my feet
Which draws closer to a truce

LUZ

Para Son de palmas de Elena Laura

Explotan las sílabas
Amarillas entre las manos
El sol suena

Las siento en el pecho
Las siento en el vientre
Las siento, las siento, las siento

Sol sin miedo
Das calor
Cubres el cuerpo

Sílabas de luz
Que cobijan
Que dan seguridad

Del son de palmas
Nace la luz
Luz de Andalucía

La siento, la siento
La siento, la siento
La siento, la luz

LIGHT

After Son de palmas by Elena Laura

Yellow syllables erupt
In-between these hands
The sun echoes

I sense these syllables in my chest
I sense them in my midriff
I sense them, sense them, sense them

Sun without fright
You provide heat
You flood my body

Syllables of light
Which shelter
Which grant refuge

From resonance of these palms,
Light is born
Andalucian light

I sense; I sense
I sense; I sense
I sense this light

Xánath Caraza

LAST BLUE MOON

Para la pintura de Steven Kalaher

Aves anaranjadas que brillan en el cielo de la noche guiándose
por marineros en las ciudades sin océanos
Pájaros siguiendo la última luna llena del calendario maya
Ciudad de trigo dorado que susurra poemas olvidados entre
tornados de fuego
Poemas que crecen en las ramas de los álamos y esparcen sus
sonidos
En olas de las praderas verdes, nuestros océanos de sabiduría,
nuestras voces ancestrales
Búfalos perdidos, marineros perdidos persiguiendo la luna azul
en los cielos abiertos de la noche
Corazones perdidos siguiendo sonidos de sabiduría
Corazones palpitantes buscando la libertad en las praderas verdes
Blue moon you left them standing alone
Océanos verdes de marineros perdidos

LAST BLUE MOON

After the painting by Steven Kalaher

Orange birds shining in the night sky guiding lost sailors among oceanless cities
Birds following the last blue moon of the Mayan calendar
City of golden wheat whispering forgotten poems with tornadoes of fire in between
Poems that grow on branches of the cottonwood tree and spread their sounds
In waves of dark green prairies, our oceans of wisdom, our ancestral voices
Lost buffalos, lost sailors following the blue moon in open skies of the night
Los hearts following sounds of wisdom
Beating hearts looking for freedom in the green prairies
Blue moon you left them standing alone
Green ocean of lost sailors.

Xánath Caraza

NOCTURNO

Para Superstition Mountain por Tom Weso Pecore

Recuerdos de filigrana de plata
Sobre las dunas del desierto
Noche morada que hiela el corazón
Luz negra que absorben los cactus
Efímera eternidad
Música nocturna
Viento del desierto
Sentimientos violetas en la vista
Los recuerdos se borran
Con la luz cegadora

NOCTURNE

After Superstition Mountain by Tom Weso Pecore

Silver, filigreed memories
On top of desert dunes of the
Purple night that freezes the heart
Black light cacti absorb
Ephemeral eternity
Nocturnal music
Desert wind
Violet feelings in sight
Memories fade
With blinding light

Xánath Caraza

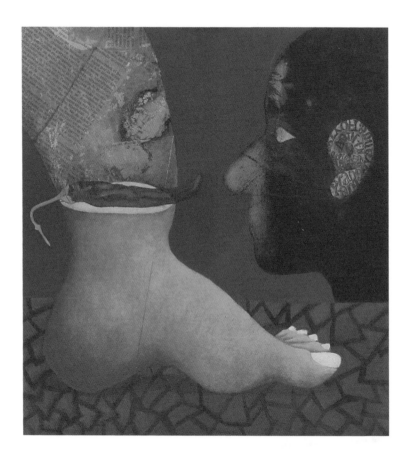

YANGA

Para Louis Reyes Rivera
Este poema inspiró El sueño de Yanga por Adriana Manuela

Yanga, Yanga, Yanga,
Yanga, Yanga, Yanga,
Hoy, tu espíritu invoco
Aquí, en este lugar.

Este, este es mi poema para Yanga,
Mandinga, malanga, bamba.
Rumba, mambo, samba,
Palabras llegadas de África.

Esta, esta es mi respuesta para Yanga,
Candomble, mocambo, mambo,
Candomble, mocambo, mambo,
Hombre libre veracruzano.

En 1570
Llegaste al puerto de Veracruz,
Encadenado como muchos,
Escapaste de la esclavitud.

Palenque, rumba, samba,
Yanga, Yanga, Yanga,
Espíritu indomable,
Noble hombre de África.

En 1609
Luchaste por la libertad,
Hasta tus puertas llegaron y
No pudieron entrar.

Mandinga, malanga, bamba,
Palenque, rumba, samba,
Palenque, rumba, samba,

Orgullo, ritmo y libertad.

Para 1630
San Lorenzo de los Negros
Se estableció.
Hoy, el pueblo de Yanga.

Candomble, mocambo, mambo,
Yanga, Yanga, Yanga,
Hoy, tu espíritu invoco
Aquí, en este lugar.

Yanga, Yanga, Yanga,
Palenque, rumba, samba,
Mandinga, malanga, bamba,
Candomble, mocambo, mambo.

Candomble, mocambo, mambo,
Mandinga, malanga, bamba,
Palenque, rumba, samba,
Yanga, Yanga, Yanga.

YANGA

For Louis Reyes Rivera
This poem inspired El sueño de Yanga by Adriana Manuela

Yanga, Yanga, Yanga
Yanga, Yanga, Yanga
Today, your spirit I invoke
Here, in this place

This, this is my poem for Yanga
Mandinga, malanga, bamba
Rumba, mambo, samba.
Words having arrived from Africa

This, this is my answer for Yanga
Candomble, mocambo, mambo
Candomble, mocambo, mambo
Free man of Veracruz

In 1570
You arrived at the Port of Veracruz
In chains as many
You escaped slavery

Palenque, rumba, samba
Yanga, Yanga, Yanga
Unconquerable spirit
Noble man from Africa

In 1609
You fought for freedom
At your doors, they arrived and
They couldn't come in

Mandinga, malanga, bamba
Palenque, rumba, samba
Palenque, rumba, samba

Pride, rhythm and freedom

By 1630
San Lorenzo de los negros
Was established
Today, the town of Yanga

Candomble, mocambo, mambo
Yanga, Yanga, Yanga
Today, your spirit I invoke
Here, in this place

Yanga, Yanga, Yanga
Palenque, rumba, samba
Mandinga, malanga, bamba
Candomble, mocambo, mambo

Condomble, mocambo, mambo
Mandinga, malanga, bamba
Palenque, rumba, samba
Yanga, Yanga, Yanga.

BERMEJAS ESCAMAS

Para Aqua de Elena Laura

Contenido en el agua
Aguarda el pez
De bermejas escamas

Espera en el hielo
De la memoria carmín
Con la vida suspendida

Arriba, el exuberante manglar
Bloquea la luz del sol
El pez aguanta la respiración

Se detiene la fluidez
En el agua, la roja palabra
Se ensarta en la boca del pez

Mientras desde el manglar
Una imprevista gota se desliza
La esperanza de vivir

Sin aviso arrasa las bermejas escamas
Del pez la caudalosa corriente de
Sonidos acuáticos del corazón

VERMILLION SCALES

After Aqua by Elena Laura

Meaning in the water
Vermillion scaled
Fish pauses

Lingering in the ice
Of crimson memory
While life is suspended

From above, lush mangrove
Thwarts sunlight
Fish enduring its breathing

Gracefulness at a standstill
Water-bound, reddish word
Spears the fish's mouth

Meanwhile, from the mangrove,
A candid droplet slips down
Hope to live

Without warning, it smoothes back its vermillion scales
From the fish, mighty current of
watery sounds of the heart

Xánath Caraza

DELATA

Para Aguanta corazón de Aster

La emoción no ocultas
Corazón delator del
Hombre venado

Perdido entre la selva
Rotas las cadenas
Liberado de mí

Corazón palpitante
En la mente te tengo
Siempre te veo

Corazón en las ramas
Oscuridad de palabras
Abierto estás a vibrar

Venado hombre, niño venado
Venado hambriento de amor
Corazón lleno de deseo

El ansia es más grande
El corazón delata
Tu intimidad

WEARING YOUR HEART

After Aguanta Corazón by Aster

You conceal not your feelings
Deerman's heart
giving him away

Nowhere to be found amid the wilderness
Chains are broken
Liberated of me

Beating heart
You are on my mind
I look on you, always

Heart within the branches
Gloominess of words
You are open to resonating

Deerman, deerchild
Deer starving for love
Heart filled with longing

This yearning is boundless
Your heart is wearing
Your intimacy

Xánath Caraza

SONIDO

Para The Coming of Venus de Heriberto Luna

Azules ondas emergen
Desde lo profundo del cuerpo
Turquesa vibrante
A través de la garganta

La trémula piel se enciende
Tornándose en atardecer
La mano alcanza al cielo lapislázuli
Con llama de fuego nuevo

Atuendo bordado de luna
Lleno de luz y firmamento
Viajes remotos en la mirada
Cielo grabado en la falda

La flamígera estrella
Atraviesa los ojos
Y luego ya nadie
La puede sacar

SOUND

After The Coming of Venus by Heriberto Luna

Blue waves transpire
From the depths of her body
Shuttering turquoise
From within her throat

Trembling skin ignites
Meandering into twilight
Her hand stretches to the lapis lazuli sky
With a blaze of new fire

Garb embroidered with moon eyes
Filled with light and firmly
Remote journeys in her eyesight
Sky engraved into her skirt

Burning star
Pierces her eyes
And it follows that not a soul
is capable, in the end, of luring it out

Xánath Caraza

ESTREMECIMIENTO

Para Sacra líbido de Elena Laura

Se impregna de niebla la piel
Los párpados ceden al calor, luz del atardecer
El roce sutil se transforma en dorado aliento
Sístole, música interna, ritmos de la sangre

Penetra la humedad, explotan sílabas de la noche en el paladar
Pausada lectura de la poesía corporal
Suaves arabescos entre pulsaciones exhalo
La sangre se desliza en el cuerpo con intensidad

Ritmos internos de un instante, delicadeza
Inhalo fuerza, diástole azul, lentamente
La pasión de otra piel se intuye
Estremecimiento en el flamígero amanecer

GOOSEBUMPS

After Sacra líbido by Elena Laura

Their skin is bathed in mist
Their eyelids succumb to the heat, twilight
Their subtle touch motions into a gilded sigh
Palpating heart, inward music, rhythms of blood

Moisture seeps in, nighttime syllables on the palate burst
Intervals of incarnate poetry reading
Soft, intricate and intertwining artistry amid a pulse of exhaling
Blood runs down their bodies with fervor

Inward rhythms for an instant, gracefulness
I breathe vigor in, slow bluish expansion of the heart
The craze of another skin is felt
Goosebumps at opulent dawn

ABOUT THE AUTHOR

Xánath Caraza is a traveler, educator, poet and short story writer. Caraza is an Award Winning Finalist in the 'Fiction: Multicultural' category of the 2013 International Book Awards. Her book Conjuro was awarded second place in the 'Best Poetry Book in Spanish' category and received honorable mention in the 'Best First Book in Spanish, Mariposa Award' category of the 2013 International Latino Book Awards. She was named number one of the 2013 Top Ten "New" Latino Authors to Watch (and Read) by LatinoStories.com. She won the 2003 Ediciones Nuevo Espacio international short story contest in Spanish and was a 2008 finalist for the first international John Barry Award. Originally from Xalapa,Veracruz, Mexico, she has lived in Vermont and Kansas City. She has an M.A. in Romance Languages. She lectures in Foreign Languages and Literatures at the University of Missouri-Kansas City. Her upcoming poetry collection, Sílabas de viento (2014) is from Mammoth Publications. Her short story collection, Lo que trae la marea/ What the Tide Brings (2013) is from Mouthfeel Press. Her full-length book of poetry Conjuro (2012) is from Mammoth Publications and her chapbook Corazón Pintado: Ekphrastic Poems (2012) is from TL Press. Caraza writes the US Latino Poets en español column and the poetry/narrative section in Revista Zona de Ocio. She curates the National Poetry Month, Poem-a-Day project, for the Con Tinta Literary Organization since 2012. Caraza has participated in Festival Latinoamericano de Poesía de New York City de 2013, X Festival Internacional de Poesía de la ciudad de Granada, Andalucía, España de 2013, Floricanto Barcelona 2011 and 2012, Festival de Flor y Canto 2010, USC. Caraza is an advisory circle member of the Con Tinta literary organization and a former board member of the Latino Writers Collective in Kansas City. She has taught in Mexico, Brazil, China, Spain and the US. Her Day of the Dead Art work has been exhibited at the Nelson Atkins Museum of Art, Kansas City, MO.

ARTISTS AND TRANSLATOR

Adriana Manuela

Paraadriana69@gmail.com

www.facebook.com/adrianamanuelastudio

Adriana Manuela is a painter and ceramist originally from Mexico. She has participated in individual shows in Mexico, Spain and Germany among other countries. Currently, she lives in Córdoba, Andalusia, Spain. Adriana Manuela is working on a new series of ceramics titled: Yolotl.

Aster

Aster is a young emerging artist from Chiapas, Mexico. He is a student of Juan Chawuk. El repertorio temático de su obra está relacionado con la realidad de vidas humanas e inhumanas, propias y ajenas, buscando la forma de entendernos como seres sociales viviendo el arte. Su nombre verdadero es Cristian Mauricio Espinosa González

Elena Laura

http://www.elenalaura.com/

Elena Laura is a painter and printer from Granada, Andalusia, Spain. She also works serigraphy and artistic typography. Elena Laura has had over thirty individual shows and over seventy collective shows all over Spain, Germany, France, Denmark, New York City, Miami and Tokio. She is also the editor of "Poesía en el Jardín: Revista de Poesía".

Heriberto Luna

hluna2525@yahoo.com

Heriberto Luna is a painter and tattoo artist from Los Angeles, CA. Luna is originally from Mexico and has exhibited in twenty major Museums, among them such prestigious locations as: The Santa Monica Museum of Art, The National Mexican Fine art Museum in Illinois and The Museum of History and Art in Ontario, California. Beyond that, Luna's works have become part of major art collections at Arizona State University and in 2006 Los Angeles Mayor Antonio Villaraigosa presented him with an award of recognition for his accomplishments in the arts; Luna has also been awarded two artist-in-residence grants from the Los Angeles Cultural Affairs department.

Israel Nazario

Nazario90@hotmail.com

Israel Nazario is originally from Santa María Zacatepec, Putla, Oaxaca, Mexico. He graduated from the Escuela de Bellas Artes, UABJO, in the City of Oaxaca, Oaxaca, Mexico. His work has been displayed in several collective and individual shows in Mexico, Japan, and Brazil. Currently, he lives in the city of Oaxaca where he teaches and paints.

Juan Chawuk

http://juanchawuk.com/

Juan Chawuk is a Tojolobal Maya, from Las Margaritas in Chiapas, Mexico. He is a contemporary artist and a passionate arts advocate and arts activist. Chawuk is an acclaimed and celebrated painter, sculptor, installation artist, and performance artist. His work has been featured throughout Mexico and in solo exhibits at Rutgers University, in Milwaukee, Chicago and Kansas City.

Steven Kalaher Taillbois

Steven Kalaher is a full-time art faculty member at the Otero Junior College in La Junta, CO. He teaches Art History, Drawing, Painting, Studio Art and Design. Kalaher has been featured all over the USA.

Thomas Weso

Deniselow9@hotmail.com

Thomas Weso is an educator and artist. His vivid paintings based on Woodlands motifs are in collections in Washington DC as well as the Midwest, and he has participated in solo and group shows in Kansas and Missouri. Tom is an enrolled member of the Menominee Indian Nation of Wisconsin. He teaches Native American Studies classes at Friends University. He has published personal essays and articles. He received his M.A. in Indigenous Nations Studies from the University of Kansas.

Stephen Holland-Wempe

Stephen Holland-Wempe has taught, translated, and interpreted

Spanish, French, and English. He has taught scientific translation in southern Mexico, where he was also the official translator and interpreter for the university international program. For the last twelve years, he has been at the Applied Language Institute at the University of Missouri at Kansas City, where he is the Language and Intercultural Specialist. He is currently completing his international Ph.D. in Social Sciences from the Taos Institute in the U.S. and Tilburg University in the Netherlands.